Poems
FROM THE
Heart

Kuldip Nijjar

AuthorHouse™ UK
1663 Liberty Drive
Bloomington, IN 47403 USA
www.authorhouse.co.uk
UK TFN: 0800 0148641 (Toll Free inside the UK)
UK Local: 02036 956322 (+44 20 3695 6322 from outside the UK)

This book is printed on acid-free paper.

ISBN: 979-8-8230-8856-5 (sc)
ISBN: 979-8-8230-8855-8 (e)

Print information available on the last page.

Published by AuthorHouse 06/28/2024

authorHOUSE®

♥ Happiness

Happiness comes from inside
When one is content with themselves
They feel loved
Happiness is free
Happiness brings a smile on a person's
Face and makes them glow with brightness of happy feelings
Just be happy and live your life freely
the way you want it to be

♥ Feeling content

To feel happy is the best thing in the world
Do things that make you feel happy and
Not what the world expects from you
Be yourself and be happy

♥ Life

I felt good I thought the feeling will last forever
But I soon realise nothing in this life lasts forever
In life we experience good and bad times
Happiness joy and the cycle goes on and on until death and
rebirth and joy again this is the cycle of life

♥ Loneliness

Been alone is not good for the soul
Been alone gives you time to think re adjust and change
But above all love is all you need
A hug sometimes can make everything feel ok and for someone to say it's going to be OK

♥ Finding love

Wishing you a star so bright
That it glows so bright in your heart and makes you feel happy
I saw a shooting star and made a wish
That night I wished that my soul will fall in love with another two become one in love

♥ Emotions

It's ok to cry get them emotions out your mind
It's better out, than in breath and tell yourself everything is going to be OK

♥ Belonging

When you have a sense of belonging
It helps you feel secure
Family friends bring love
Into your life
A love that can last a lifetime that money can never buy

🖤 Being strong

You have to be strong in life and not let people control you and put you down.
Don't let people walk all over you be a lion

🖤 Seeing love

You make me smile and you just don't
Realise how much you mean to me
I would pick up the moon and stars for you that's how much
Your love to me means beyond the earth
Destined soul mates forever

You deserve to get everything you need and more in this life
Seeing you be happy and content will also make me happy

🖤 Cherishing love

If you join two ears together they create a shape of a heart
How beautiful it is when you meet your lover and how two hearts beating fall in love

🖤 Relationships

We was once two peas in a pod
It's sad when the blood relationship is torn apart over money anger and pride
But the sweetest thing is when you both admit to your mistakes
So in time your relationships stores and in time you can create
beautiful memories again that you can cherish forever

💗 Finding love

Listen to your lover whispering in your ear
It's so sweet is sounds pure like the ocean
His words are all sweet as honey all sloppy and gooey like the scent of nectar
How sweet and tasty it sounds
Unconditional love is when you love each other regardless of money and materialistic things
Materialistic things will come and go and will not last forever
But true love remains in your heart
Forever and ever more

💗 Inner self

Beauty is in the way of the holder it is so deep even the most beautiful girl
in the world can look ugly when her heart is not in the right place
Don't let ego pride take over your mind be nice and kind to everyone you meet

💗 Life

Life can feel like a jigsaw waiting for the missing piece to
fit the puzzle is all you may be waiting for
When it's found life will start to make sense two minds are always better than one

💗 Journey of life

I once had a scar on my arm
So I went to the tattoo shop to get stars tattooed on my arm
But I backed out, but today the scars have faded themselves.
That's what happens when you experience things in life the sad
memory fades so you can enjoy the good things in life

💗 Childhood

When I was young child I have the scars on my head
when I fell three times on the floor playing
I was stitched up and the hospital three times
These stitches saved my life and in time repaired my injuries these
scars have built me up for life and made me a stronger person

💗 Friendships

No more getting trampled on by friends family people that are unappreciative
Weakness and words can get you down if you're not careful
But sometimes harsh words can turn you strong
Make sure you stand up for what is right in life and do not let words get you down
Sticks and stones may break my bones but people's name will never hurt me

💗 Dreaming

Turn me into a butterfly singing a lullaby
Reaching to touch the sky getting ready to achieve all the dreams I wanted
I'm getting ready to spread my wings and reach high to achieve my destiny

Be a dreamer make your fairy tale become true
One day your Prince will appear in your heart and it will be a perfect love story
Remember never forget dreaming dreams can come true

 Life

What is life
Life is a bit like a box of chocolates
You do not know what you're going to get until you pick one
You don't know what flavour or texture you are going
to get or what direction life will take you
Until you choose and make a sacrifice and set yourselves goals to achieve

 Holy

The moon and stars even worship
Your holy name God
Fear has no equal to God's love
The highest formula+ %= equals love
Life is for loving
God is love

♥ Divine

God is closer than you think
Dig deep his love is within ♡
You

I will sing so loud to you God
Over the hills and far away my voice will reach you

This world needs love that makes the world go around
Love is everything and the world goes around with one love

♥ Closeness

When you feel lost and lonely
Rember you are not alone
God is right there by the broken hearted to fix your heart
Days I thought God had abandon me but he was carrying me
The days I could not walk he carried me
I just did not see his footprints but his love was always holding me higher

♥ Knowing who you are

Haters can talk crap
As I do not care no more
I know who I am in God
Love

♥ Faith restores the soul

When I was overwhelmed
God gave me grace and was holding me tight in his arms

I am not perfect but I'm better wiser and stronger
No one can take advantage of a strong person

♥ Winning

I'm a winner I am going to win
The race no matter how long it will take the tortoise won in the end
You don't have to compete with others it's your life do things right in your pace and peace

7

♥ Belonging

No more worries its time for happiness as he is making me whole
by his grace I will have victory I will be a champion

I don't want to be lonely no more
I just want to feel belonged and loved
I just want someone to be kind to me
I just want to feel hugged these simple things in life will make me feel happy
In Gods love I will find happiness
God I love you
With all my heart
Jadore
With thy whole heart I will praise you

♥ Intervention

Heavens open when you call God's holy
Name righteously within your heart
He answers your prays
And may be one day you will win that lottery ha keep praying

♥ Friendships

A strong friendship will be there beside you through happy and sad moments
A friend will always remain by your side to lift you out
the dark and will make you feel happy again

💗 Being à woman

A strong woman holds the heart to its family. Her keys of love she dwells on her family
are greater than ever she is so strong love is all she needs to be proud of her pride

💗 Strong

I got wisdom knowledge
I'm stronger than ever before
To empower me to live a better life to achieve all my goals dreams and achieve happiness
beyond all keep smiling until you get it right be patient let God's light shine in your life

I'm unshakeable unstoppable as God is greater than ever
I will be strong and achieve my goals dreams and aspirations

You are going to be strong and powerful by the end of the year victory is yours.
You are a champion for goodness

💗 Being content

A rich man builds its riches
But a poor man will give you his heart and show you compassion
What will you choose in the path of life
Be greedy and be rich
Or stay humble and remain simple

♥ Being strong

What did not break me will make me stronger
You are going to strengthen me like the wings of a Eagle
Fly high to achieve the dreams you are wanting to achieve
The dreams you are wanting to succeed
Do what makes you feel happy and good in life and don't follow what others want you to be

♥ Achieving

I am going to achieve something I never thought I could
do and it don't have to be something big.
Something small can equally make u happy.my dream is to take a air balloon ride
I will ride over the hills and sky's so far away I'm flying with
God by my side there's no way I could loose

♥ We are all winners in life

It's not a race take things easy in your pride you don't
have to compete with others to achieve

♥ Emotions

If I did not feel pain
I would not have been a poet
Writing helps you express yourself from
Your good and bad moments in life they mould you and you learn to embrace
the journey of life that one day your words may lift someone else in life

❤ The language of love

Red is the colour of love
Red is for passion
Red is for a rose
That brings a sweet scent to your life with a passion of striving for love

❤ Life's mysteries

Life what is life
Life is a mystery with many choices you never know what road
you will take until you pick the right destination in life

❤ Being nice

Don't judge me as you need to look at yourself first
You're not perfect so just be nice to one another

❤ Nature

A bird makes me feel free because they can spread there
wings and fly to any destination they want
Oh how it must feel to be high in the sky

❤ Relationships

There is power in connection
Connection leads to life in relationships
With loved ones
Connections open doors to your destiny to bring you joy in life

♥ Life quote

Health is wealth appreciate this
No money in the world can buy your health back take time for yourself

♥ True friends

A fake friend will tell you
You can not do that and fill yourself with disbelief
A real friend will tell you it might take time to achieve but anything is possible through life
The real friend will wait patiently for you and will always be
at your side through good and bad moments.
That is a true friend

♥ Love

When I looked into your eyes for the first time
I saw stars sparkling into your eyes
My body felt all mellow and yellow the brightness made my heart shine with your love

♥ Changing times

They say that time is à Healer time makes things better
Time changes things
Time is a healer you experience happy and sad times in this life
Time make everything feel new again be patient

♥ Good people

The right people in your life
Will come divine interventions
There become a atmosphere shift it creates happy moments
That's how time can heal and change your life.
We need to attract good people to help the heart
When the heart feels fulfilled
Everything changes your whole mind body and soul feels new

♥ Hope

Do you know the best thing in life is Free that is love
Picking up a flower from the garden and giving it someone is an act of purity and love

♥ Motivating

If your heart is beating and you still have life in you. There's
still time to achieve your dreams nothings too late

♥ Compassion

God my trust is in you
Please guard my heart and shut the mouths of liars in my life
Make them so busy that there gossip confuses there own selves

♥ Having hope

They say don't loose heart
But it's the mind that you got to control
As the mind gives a signal to the heart
The mind is the most powerful tool that a human can visualise the mind
can help you achieve things you need to make your dreams possible

♥ Dreaming big

If you get taught right in life
These teachings make you realise you can achieve anything in this
life it is possible to dream big and make that dream a reality

♥ Love

I will dive in the ocean
Finding your love in slow motion we shall fall in love and
find the pearls of the ocean floating together

♥ Life quotes

The breath and life you
Have is a gift from God
Make the most of it
FAITH
No one can ever stop what you started God
No one can take your place God
God had not lost one battle to date there's one love that saves us all

♥ Life

Everything truly happens for a reason
Sometimes life brings you happiness and peace sometimes life is just hard
But all things happen for a season it's all for the right reason

♥ Believing

You who believe in angels they belong to God
The sun makes you feel better you know well that's just
God's healing in your life to help you feel better

♥ Small circles

You will not be loved by everyone in life
This is just how life works
But if you are lucky to find a few good people who love you in life that is all you need
Keep that circle small

♥ Love keeps you going

Love is the solution to the higher power
Love makes everything OK
Love is the best antidote
Love has companion on one souls
Love makes you happy
Love makes you smile
Love has no pride
Love makes you patient
Your love is beautiful like the stars in the sky

Karma

Karma no need for revenge just sit back relax quietly
They say what comes around goes around
Those words that hurt you one day God will bring justice and
allow you to see what goes around comes around.

Divine

God is so loving
God is so kind
God is the Master of the universe
With God you can climb mountains
With God you can conqueor
With God all things are possible

Restoration

Rain rain go away come back another day
God make it rain tomorrow With tears of joy and happiness
As you have opened up the Heaven
God then let the SUNSHINE on all the righteous in the world let them feel your love

❤ Being humble

Please God always keep me humble
Please God keep my mind on you
Please God guide my footsteps and make my future bright and healthy

❤ Motivation

If you get some happiness in life it restores your faith
and keeps you motivated to achieve things
Please God bring peace and happiness in my life

❤ Love

I love you so much if I could reach the stars for you
I would put one in your heart
So our love will sparkle forever and ever
The warmth of your love is like the heat of the sun so bright That our love will
shine together through good times and bad times I will always be by your side
Like à cloud we will lift each other higher to reach the sky
there's no limits and our love will remain forever

🖤 Friendships

A friend is always there for you in the walk of life
A true friend will always be by your side through moments of joy laughter
sadness happiness these unforgetable moments will always be cherished

Do you remember times when you were so young you get drunk like a skunk.
You lie on your friend shoulders when you're so out of your mind they pull you
out the dark shadow hold your hand and will always be there for you
A good friend will never leave you alone
You go through sorrows and pain and your friend will always be there to lift you up
A friend is like an Angel in the sky who understands your soul
A true friend will never judge you they will come running
to your defence to always support you
You travel around the world together you see the beauty of the world you
dance into the dawn partying it feels like you are in paradise
I will always be there for you my friend we will lift each other higher to reach the sky
We do silly things we follow our heart we are like two peas in a pod.
Our friendship is à bond so strong it will remain forever more.

🖤 Higher Power

Oh higher spirit in the sky come and show me your love the love you promise like no
one can give.I want to feel the touch of your higher power so mighty and strong
Come into my life and change my life .How I long to feel your holy touch
you are the greatest love of all no one can ever take your place.
You are the Diamond of my life I want to feel you in my soul
come and bring me a new life full of your love.
I do not want to feel pain anymore God you promise not to leave my side

Please wash away these tears stop my river flowing with floods
but let my floods of tears be filled with love and peace.

❤ Liars

I hate liars there decietful people there tounge is like a snake, they
will rob you until they get what they want from you.
They leave you dry and rob you of your treasures. Liars are
decietful people just like the snake tempted eve
A liars lips and word are so sweet like honey they manipulate
you .Once they have taken everything away from you they move onto
the next victim there next target there new pride of kittens.
Watch out for liars in your life they come like a Thief in the dark. Put your
armorial of bravery on and guard your heart and mind always.

❤ God's beauty

Gods love is so pure that I can not even describe
When I think of love I think of God
God is holy untouchable unshakeable unbreakable
His works we will never know, he created beauty. Beauty like the pearls in the ocean.
Your forever loyal God, you're the best companion that I can ever have.
You put the sun in the sky and gave it light
You put the moon in the sky and darkness comes but
your beauty remains forever In this world
You put the stars in the sky so they twinkle so bright .The
flowers grow and u give them à pure scent of smell.
You have created so many beautiful things you are our
ABBA father the one who listens to our hearts.
You make the black birds become white you can do everything you want God, I will never
know your works and mysterious ways. I will praise you with my heart Forever more.

🖤 Acceptance

Do not think my niceness is going to make me change for you.
Accept the people in your life for who they are.
Accept you for who you are.
Do not let the world get you down dont let the world change you. You
do not have to change yourself to fit in dont be fake to yourself.
To make it in life and be happy shut the door on people who try and change you.
Do not let the fakeness in your life in
be true to yourself have confidence and feel loved

🖤 My ocean of peace

You're my ocean
Ocean so calm and tender
I see the tranquil colour blue it fills my lungs with peace I feel im on the moon
I feel the seas tides wash away my pains im so white and pure like a snow fake
Like the river flowing the nile your love pours inside my soul
It feels my soul has been lifted in the arms of an Angel the wings around me I feel so safe
Ohh my ocean sing me a song that's so nice and sweet you are
my ocean that keeps me so calm tender and so sweet.
I feel like I am hypnotised in the calmness of your peace I swim deeper in
the ocean I feeling peace I never want to come out im lost in time.

♥ Fooliness

You took me for a fool you made me belive your love was
pure. But all you ever wanted was to use me.
I was never good enough all you wanted was the pocket of my money
I'm not the fool for you, you are the fool because you blew
away your chances to something really beautful.
You fooled your own heart you will never find this true love again
Now move yourself away from my life
The fool in life will eventually see karma will bite them
like a bee it will Sting you back one day.
Treat people the way you want to be treated

♥ Love

Love is the solution to the higher power
Love makes everything okay
Love is the best antidote
Love has companion on ones soul
Love makes you happy
Love makes you smile
Love has no pride
Love is beautful like the stars in the sky

Printed in the United States
by Baker & Taylor Publisher Services